Jackie Joyner-Kersee

Track-And-Field Star

Carol Fuchs

illustrations by Teri Rider

The Rourke Corporation, Inc.   Vero Beach, Florida

© 1993 by The Rourke Corporation, Inc.

All rights reserved. No part of this book may be reproduced or utilized in any form or by any means, electronic or mechanical including photocopying, recording, or by any information storage and retrieval system without permission in writing from the publisher.

The Rourke Corporation, Inc.
P.O. Box 3328, Vero Beach, FL 32964

Series Editor: Gregory Lee
Production: The Creative Spark, San Clemente, CA

Library of Congress Cataloging-in-Publication Data

Fuchs, Carol A.
    Jackie Joyner-Kersee, track-and-field star / by Carol Fuchs.
       p. cm. — (Reaching your goal)
    Summary: A biography of the track and field champion who has won Olympic gold medals in both the long jump and the heptathlon.
    ISBN 0-86593-261-1
    1. Joyner-Kersee, Jacqueline, 1962- —Juvenile literature. 2. Track and field athletes—United States—Biography—Juvenile literature. 3. Women track and field athletes—United States—Biography—Juvenile literature. [1. Joyner-Kersee, Jacqueline, 1962- 2. Track and field athletes. 3. Afro-Americans—Biography.] I. Title. II. Series.
GV697.J69F83 1993
796.42'092—dc20
[B]   92-45244
                                                                       CIP
                                                                        AC

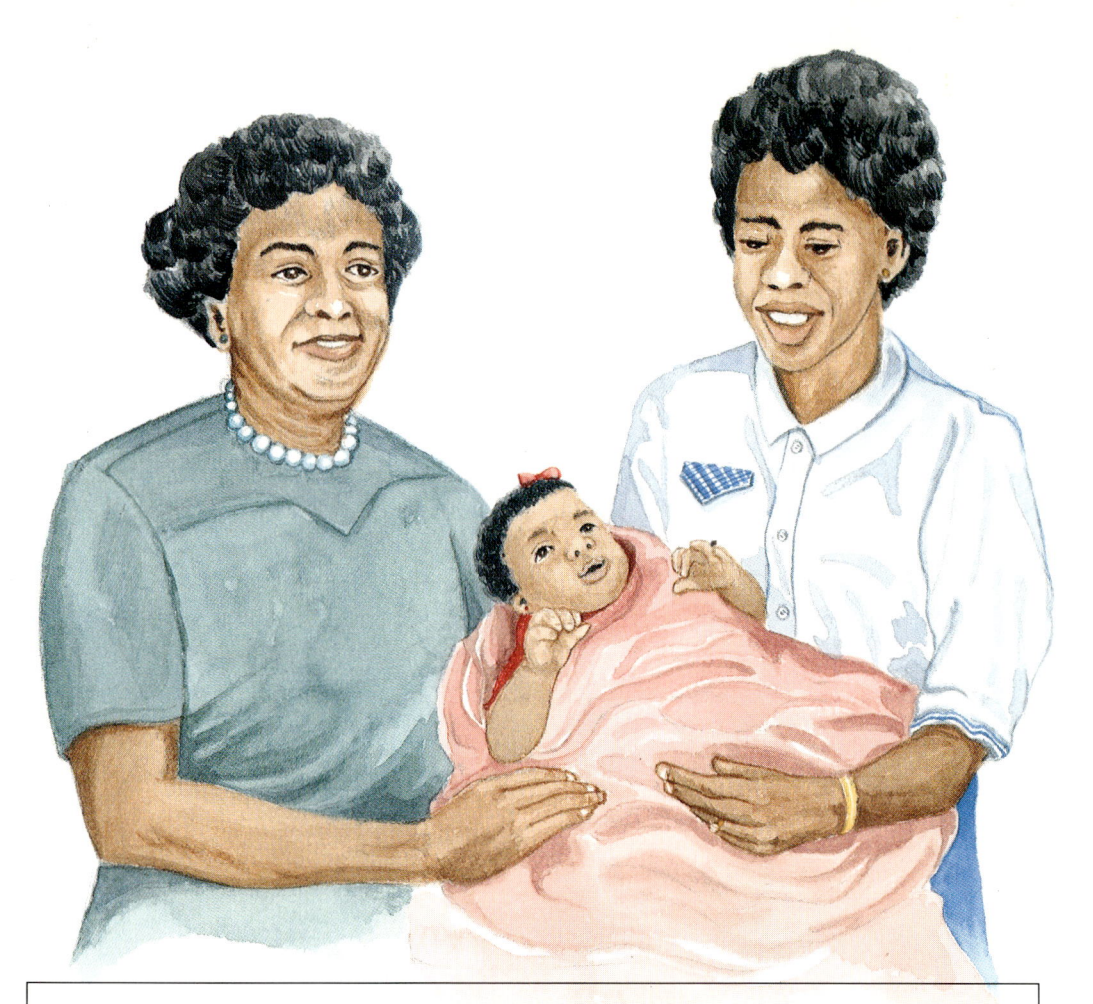

On March 3, 1962, a baby girl was born in East St. Louis, Illinois. She was named Jacqueline after Jacqueline Kennedy. Kennedy was married to President John F. Kennedy. That made her the first lady. The baby girl's grandmother insisted on the name. She was sure great things would happen to baby Jacqueline. "Someday this girl will be the first lady of something," her grandmother said.

Jackie's parents were named Alfred and Mary Joyner. They and their four children lived in a small house. It was not elegant. In the winter the hot-water pipes froze. The family had to heat bath water in kettles on the stove.

Jackie's mother was a nurse's assistant. Her father worked in other cities as a construction worker. There was no work for him in East St. Louis. Once he worked as a railroad switch operator in Springfield, Illinois. That was two hours away from home.

East St. Louis was a poor town. There was a lot of crime. Young Jackie once saw someone murdered in front of her house.

Jackie worked hard at sports even as a child. "I was nine years old when I had my first track competition. I finished last." But the very next week in practice she knew she was improving.

Jackie's parents did not think track and field was a good sport for a girl. They tried to convince her to give it up. But Jackie believed in what she was doing. By her third competition she had won three second-place finishes. And then one day she came home and said, "I got five first places, Daddy." After that her parents stopped trying to keep little Jackie from competing.

By the time Jackie was 12 years old she could long jump more than 17 feet. She was so good at sports her brother Al wanted to compete as well. He became a winner in the triple jump.

8

Jackie worked hard in the classroom, too. She enjoyed doing the best she could. In the fifth grade her hardest subject was long division. Jackie did not understand it at first. So she worked at it just as hard as she worked at track. Before long she was sitting in the front of the class with the other good students.

When she was 14 years old Jackie won her first National Junior Pentathlon championship. To win she had to compete in five running, throwing and jumping events. She won the pentathlon every year for the next three years.

In high school Jackie set a state record in the long jump. She jumped more than 20 feet. She also played volleyball and basketball. Jackie became known as the best young athlete in Illinois.

In 1980 she graduated. Many colleges wanted Jackie. She accepted a basketball scholarship for UCLA. Soon, she became a star forward for the UCLA Bruins basketball team.

During Jackie's first year at UCLA her mother died suddenly. Jackie was grief stricken. But she remembered her mother's determination that she always do her best.

An assistant track coach named Bob Kersee comforted Jackie. Later they would marry. He saw what a great athlete Jackie could be. Bob said she should try the heptathlon. The heptathlon is made up of seven track-and-field events. Bob believed Jackie would be the world record holder.

In 1983, Jackie and her brother Al represented the U.S. in Helsinki, Finland. Jackie pulled a hamstring muscle and was in great pain. It was the first time she was so badly injured that she couldn't compete.

"I always felt before that I could overcome any physical problem," said Jackie. "Helsinki was the first time I felt my legs just couldn't go anymore."

But Jackie never gave up. One year later she and her brother both qualified for the 1984 Olympics. Al won the gold medal for the triple jump. Jackie won the silver for heptathlon.

At the Goodwill Games in 1986 Jackie became the first American woman in 50 years to hold a heptathlon world record. "I set high standards for myself, and I believe if I think positive, good things will happen," she said.

Just 26 days later Jackie went to Houston, Texas, for the U.S. Olympic Festival. She was tired from all her competitions. The weather was hot. Jackie knew she had to ignore "negative thoughts" and just keep believing in her ability. She set a new world record again. She was named "Athlete of the Year" and won the 1986 Jesse Owens Award.

In 1988, Jackie won Olympic gold medals in the heptathlon and the long jump in Seoul, Korea. She was the first athlete in 64 years to win both kinds of events in one Olympics. People were calling her the best woman athlete of all time. "I like the heptathlon," Jackie said. "It shows you what you're made of."

In Barcelona, Spain, she won the Olympic gold medal for the heptathlon again. No man or woman has ever won the gold twice in a row for that event. Many people now consider her to be the best athlete in the world.

Jackie is already training for the 1996 Olympic Games in Atlanta, Georgia. She works very hard. "I remember where I came from," Jackie said.

"If the young female sees the environment I grew up in and sees my dreams and goals come true, she will realize her dreams and goals might also come true."

Reaching Your Goal

What do you want to do? Do you want to be an astronaut? A cook? If you want something you must first set goals. Here are some steps to help you reach them.

1. Explore Your Goals

Asking questions can help you decide if reaching your goal is what you really want.
Will I be happier if I reach this goal?
Will I be healthier if I reach this goal?

2. Name Your Goals

It is harder to choose a goal if it is too general. Do you want to be "happy?"
Learn to blow up a balloon.
Learn to ride a two-wheel bicycle.
Finish a book a week.

Name the goals you want to reach.

3. Start Small
Try reaching your goal with smaller goals.
Do you want to learn to skateboard?
Try standing on it first without moving.
Do you want to build a dollhouse?
Have an adult show you how to use tools.

4. Small Goals Turn Into Big Ones
Learning to improve your spelling can be a goal.
Practice shorter words first.
Learn to use bigger words in sentences.
Enter a spelling bee.

5. Stick With It
People like Jackie Joyner-Kersee reached their goals by working hard. They didn't let others talk them out of their goals. You can do it too!

Reaching Your Goal Books

Jim Abbott Left-handed Wonder
Hans Christian Andersen A Fairy Tale Life
Cher Singer and Actress
Chris Burke He Overcame Down Syndrome
Henry Cisneros A Hard Working Mayor
Beverly Cleary She Makes Reading Fun
Bill Cosby Superstar
Roald Dahl Kids Love His Stories
Jane Goodall The Chimpanzee's Friend
Jim Henson Creator of the Muppets
Jesse Jackson A Rainbow Leader
Michael Jordan A Team Player
Ted Kennedy, Jr. A Lifetime of Challenges
Jackie Joyner-Kersee Track-and-Field Star
Ray Kroc Famous Restaurant Owner
Christa McAuliffe Reaching for the Stars
Dale Murphy Baseball's Gentle Giant
Arnold Schwarzenegger Hard Work Brought Success
Dr. Seuss We Love You
Charles Schulz Great Cartoonist
Samantha Smith Young Ambassador
Steven Spielberg He Makes Great Movies

Rourke Corporation, Inc.
P.O. Box 3328
Vero Beach, FL 32964